NIGHT SWEATS

Thom Gunn

Robert L. Barth
14 Lucas Street
Florence, Kentucky 41042

Some of these poems first appeared in *Sequoia, Times Literary Supplement, Numbers, Chicago Review, Threepenny Review,* and *Poetry.*

Copyright 1987 by Thom Gunn
ISBN 0-941150-60-7

THE MAN WITH NIGHT SWEATS

I wake up cold, I who
Prospered through dreams of heat
Wake to their residue,
Sweat, and a clinging sheet.

My flesh was its own shield:
Where it was gashed, it healed.

I grew as I explored
The body I could trust
Even while I adored
The risk that made robust,

A world of wonders in
Each challenge to the skin.

I cannot but be sorry
The given shield was cracked,
My mind reduced to hurry,
My flesh reduced and wrecked.

I have to change the bed,
But catch myself instead

Stopped upright where I am
Hugging my body to me
As if to shield it from
The pains that will go through me,

As if hands were enough
To hold an avalanche off.

TERMINAL
(J.L., August 86)

The eight years difference in age seems now
Disparity so wide between the two
That when I see the man who armoured stood
Resistant to all help however good
Now helped through day itself, eased into chairs,
Or else led step by step down the long stairs
With firm and gentle guidance by his friend,
Who loves him, through each effort to descend,
Each wavering, each attempt made to complete
An arc of movement and bring down the feet
As if with that spare strength he used to enjoy,
I think of Oedipus, old, led by a boy.

STILL LIFE
(L.H., Dec 5, 86)

I shall not soon forget
The greyish-yellow skin
To which the face had set:
Lids tight: nothing of his,
No tremor from within,
Played on the surfaces.

He still found breath, and yet
It was an obscure knack.
I shall not soon forget
The angle of his head,
Arrested and reared back
On the crisp field of bed,

Back from what he could neither
Accept, as one opposed,
Nor, as a life-long breather,
Consentingly let go,
The tube his mouth enclosed
In an astonished O.

TO ISHERWOOD DYING

It could be, Christopher, from your leafed-in house
In Santa Monica where you lie and wait
   You hear outside a sound resume
     Fitful, anonymous,
   Of Berlin fifty years ago
   As autumn days got late —
The whistling to their girls from young men who
   Stood in the deep dim street, below
Dingy facades which crumbled like a cliff,
   Behind which in a rented room
     You listened, wondering if
By chance one might be whistling up for you,
   Adding unsentimentally
    'It could not possibly be.'
Now it's a stricter vigil that you hold
And from the canyon's palms and crumbled gold
    It could be possibly
   You hear a single whistle call
      Come out
    Come out into the cold.
Courting insistent and impersonal.

         Christmas week, 1985

JVC

He concentrated, as he ought,
On fitting language to his thought
And getting all the rhymes correct,
Thus exercising intellect
In such a space, in such a fashion,
He concentrated into passion.

ACE

An AWOL sailor as he drinks
Recalls a recent joke he's heard:
He who can barely read a word
Tells me the riddle of the Sphinx.

HATCHET, THE REVIEWER

A drunkard, come to think of it,
Is janus-faced: Hatchet was too.
The man you met, charm tempering wit,
Was courteous and considerate:
When he reviewed you though, he'd switch
From gentleman to envious bitch.
And the real article? You knew
He must be one of them, but which?

JAMESIAN

Their relationship consisted
In discussing if it existed.

BARREN LEAVES

Spontaneous overflows of powerful feeling:
Wet dreams, wet dreams, in libraries congealing.

LOOKS

Those eyes appear to transmit energy
And hold it back undissipated too.
His gaze is like a star, that cannot see,
A glow so steady he directs at you
You try to be the first to look aside
— Less flattered by the appearance of attention
Than vexed by the dim stirrings thus implied
Within a mind kept largely in suspension.

Although a gaze sought out, and highly placed
By lovers and photographers, it is
Too patly overwhelming for your taste.
You step back from such mannered solemnities
To focus on his no doubt sinewy power,
His restless movements, and his bony cheek.
You have seen him in the space of one half hour
Cross a street twenty times. You have heard him speak,
Reading his work to the surprise of guests
Who find that dinner was a stratagem:
Poems in which the attracted turn to pests
If they touch him before he touches them,
In which the celebrant of an appetite
Richly fulfilled will say Get off me bitch
To one who thought she had an equal right
To her desires, — nevertheless in which
He holds you by the voice of his demands,
Which take unfaltering body on the air
As need itself, live, famished, clenched like hands
Pale at the knuckle. Then, his luminous stare,
That too. He is an actor, after all,
And it's a genuine talent he engages
In playing this one character — mean, small,
But driven like Othello by his rages
As if a passion for no matter what,
Even the self, is fully justified,
Or as if anger could repopulate
The bony city he is trapped inside.

At times he has a lover he can hurt
By bringing home the pick-ups he despises
Because they let him pick them up. Alert
Always to looks — and they must look like prizes —

He blurs further distinction, for he knows
Nothing of strength but its apparent drift,
Tending and tending, and nothing of repose
Except within his kindled gaze, his gift.

THE STEALER

I lie and live
my body's fear
something's at large
and coming near

No deadbolt
can keep it back
A worm of fog
leaks through a crack

From the darkness
as before
it grows to body
in my door

Like a taker
scarved and gloved
it steals this way
like one I loved

Fear stiffens me
and a slow joy
at the approach
of the sheathed boy

Will he too do
what that one did
unlock me first
open the lid

and reach inside
with playful feel
all the better
thus to steal

NASTURTIUM

Born in a sour waste lot
You labored up to light,
Bunching what strength you'd got
And running out of sight
Through a knot-hole at last,
To come forth into sun
As if without a past,
Done with it, re-begun.

Now street-side of the fence
You take a few green turns,
Nimble in nonchalance
Before your first flower burns.
From poverty and prison
And undernourishment
A prodigal has risen,
Self-spending, never spent.

Irregular yellow shell
And drooping spur behind...
Not rare but beautiful
— Street-handsome — as you wind
And leap, hold after hold,
A golden runaway
Still running, strewing gold
From side to side all day.

PATCH WORK

The bird book says, common, conspicuous.
This time of year all day
The mocking bird
Sweeps at a moderate height
Above the densely flowering
Suburban plots of May,
The characteristic shine
Of white patch cutting through the curved ash-grey
That bars each wing;
Or it appears to us
Perched on the post that ends a washing-line
To sing there, as in flight,
A repertoire of songs that it has heard
— From other birds, and others of its kind —
Which it has recombined
And made its own, especially one
With a few separate plangent notes begun
Then linking trills as a long confident run
Toward the immediate distance,
Repeated all day through
In the sexual longings of the spring
(Which also are derivative)
And almost mounting to
Fulfilment, thus to give
Such muscular vigor to a note so strong,
Fulfilment that does not destroy
The original, still-unspent
Longings that led it where it went
But links them in a bird's inhuman joy
Lifted upon the wing
Of that patched body, that insistence
Which fills the gardens up with headlong song.